STATE REPORTS

Northern
New England

MAINE ★ NEW HAMPSHIRE ★ VERMONT

By

Thomas G. Aylesworth
Virginia L. Aylesworth

CHELSEA HOUSE PUBLISHERS

New York   Philadelphia

Created and produced by Blackbirch Graphics, Inc.
DESIGN: *Richard S. Glassman*
PROJECT EDITOR: *Elizabeth Miles Montgomery*

Library of Congress Cataloging-in-Publication Data

Aylesworth, Thomas G.
  Northern New England : Maine, New Hampshire, Vermont / by Thomas G. Aylesworth,
Virginia L. Aylesworth.

  (State reports)
  Includes bibliographical references.
  Summary: Discusses the geographical, historical, and cultural aspects of Maine, Vermont, and
New Hampshire, using maps, illustrated fact spreads, and other illustrated material to highlight the
land, history, and people of each individual state.

  ISBN 0-7910-1037-6   0-7910-1384-7 (pbk.)
  1. New England—Juvenile literature. 2. Maine—Juvenile literature. 3. Vermont—Juvenile
literature. 4. New Hampshire—Juvenile literature [1. New England. 2. Maine. 3. Vermont.
4. New Hampshire.] I. Aylesworth, Virginia. L. II. Title. III. Series: Aylesworth, Thomas G.
State reports.
F4.3.A95   1990   89-70846
974—dc20   35171   CIP
                                                                                  AC

Contents

Maine

New Hampshire

Vermont

Maine

The state seal of Maine was adopted in 1820. In the center is a pine tree that is flanked by a farmer and a seaman, representing the two chief occupations of the state. A moose lies at the foot of the tree, and over the tree is the North Star and the state motto, "Dirigo." At the bottom of the seal is the name *Maine*.

State Flag

The state flag of Maine was adopted in 1909 and contains the state seal on a field of blue—the same blue that is found in the flag of the United States.

Maine also has a merchant marine flag. On a field of white, *Dirigo* is written in blue letters. Beneath that is a pine tree around which is twined a blue anchor. Below the tree and anchor is the name *Maine* printed in blue.

State Motto

Dirigo

This motto, which means "I direct" or "I lead" in Latin repeats the idea of the North Star, an important navigational guide, on the state seal.

The Maine coast near Bar Harbor attracts many tourists.

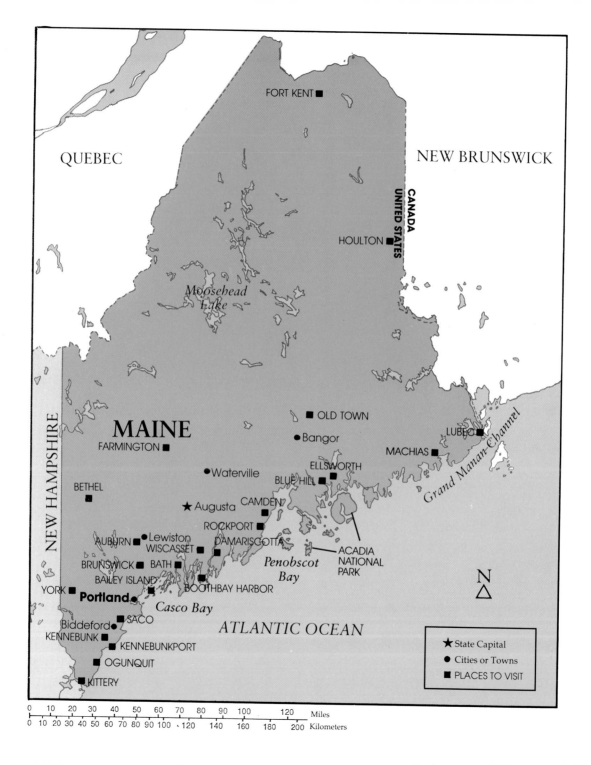

The capitol building in Augusta.

State Capital

When Maine became a state, the first capital was Portland—from 1820 to 1832. In 1832 Augusta became the capital. The statehouse was designed by Charles Bulfinch and was completed in 1832 on a 34-acre plot of land. Made of Hallowell granite, it cost $139,000, and that included the land and the furnishings. A three-story wing was added in 1890-91, and the dome with its statue of Wisdom was added in 1909-10.

9

The chickadee is the state bird.

State Name and Nicknames

No one really knows where the name of the state of Maine came from. There are those who think that early French explorers named it after the French province of Maine. On the other hand, *main* was a common word used by explorers to mean "mainland."

Maine is often called the *Pine Tree State*, since pines are so common in its 17 million acres of forests. It is also called the *Lumber State* because of the importance of that industry, and the *Border State* because it is bordered by Canada. Another nickname is *Old Dirigo* because of its motto.

The cone and tassel of the white pine is the state flower.

State Flower

The cone and tassel of the white pine, *Pinus strobus*, was named the state flower of Maine in 1895.

State Tree

Pinus strobus, the eastern white pine, was named the official tree of Maine in 1959.

State Bird

The chickadee, *Penthestes atricapillus*, became the state bird of Maine in 1927.

State Animal

The moose, *Alces americanus*, was named the state animal of Maine in 1979.

State Cat

In 1985 the Maine coon cat was named state cat.

State Fish

The landlocked salmon, *Salmo salar sebago*, was adopted as the state fish in 1969.

State Fossil

Pertica quadrifaria, an ancient plant, was named the state fossil in 1985.

State Insect

The honeybee, *Apis mellifera*, became the state insect in 1975.

State Mineral

Tourmaline has been the state mineral since 1971.

State Song

"State of Maine Song," with words and music by Roger Vinton Snow, is the official song of the state.

The Maine coon cat is the state cat.

Population

The population of Maine in 1987 was 1,187,000, making it the 38th most populous state. There are 35.7 people per square mile—approximately 47.5 percent of them in towns and cities. Almost all of the people of Maine were born in the United States. Although most of the population is of English or Scots-Irish descent, many residents, especially in the northern part of the state, are French Canadians.

A moose in a lake in northern Maine browses on aquatic plants, one of its favorite foods.

Geography and Climate

Bounded on the north by the Canadian province of New Brunswick, on the east by New Brunswick and the Atlantic Ocean, on the south by the Atlantic Ocean, and on the west by New Hampshire and the Canadian province of Quebec, Maine has an area of 33,265 square miles, making it the 39th largest state. In the north the climate is harsh in winter, but in the south and along the coast it is somewhat milder.

The Appalachian Mountains extend through the state, and are particularly rugged along the western border. There are sandy beaches along the Atlantic coast on the south, but toward the north the coastline is marked by rocky promontories, peninsulas, and fjords. The highest point in the state is on Mount Katahdin, at 5,268 feet. The lowest point is at sea level along the Atlantic coast. The major waterways in Maine are the Penobscot, Androscoggin, and Saco rivers. Moosehead Lake is the largest lake in the state.

Industries

The principal industries of the state are manufacturing, tourism, finance, insurance, and construction. The chief products are paper and wood articles, electrical and electronics products, leather goods, and boats.

The harvest of sweet corn represents an important part of Maine's agriculture.

A lobsterman in Boothbay harbor uses wooden traps not much different from those used in the early days of the colony.

Agriculture

The chief crops of the state are potatoes, hay, apples, blueberries, and sweet corn. Maine is also a livestock state, and there are estimated to be some 135,000 cattle; 79,000 hogs and pigs; 17,000 sheep; and 4.9 million chickens, geese, and turkeys on its farms. Pine, spruce, and fir timber are harvested; sand, gravel, and crushed stone are important mineral products. Commercial fishing including lobstering brings in some $108.7 million each year.

Government

The governor is the only Maine executive elected directly by the people of the state and serves a four-year term. The state legislature, which meets every other year, has a 35-member senate and a 151-member house of representatives. These legislators are elected from each of the state's counties, which send from one to five senators and three to 28 representatives to the capital, depending on the population of the county. The state constitution was adopted in 1819. In addition to its two U.S. senators, Maine has two representatives in the U.S. House of Representatives. The state has four votes in the electoral college.

History

Before the Europeans arrived, Indians of the Abenaki and Passamaquoddy tribes of the Algonkian Indian family lived in what was to become the state of Maine. The Abenaki lived in the west, and the Passamaquoddy were in the east. They had villages, but they were also nomads at times. They were a peaceful people who were often raided by the warlike Iroquois.

The first Europeans to visit the area may have been the Vikings, led by Leif Ericson, who probably arrived about

Sebastian Cabot (pictured here) and his father John Cabot, Italian explorers employed by the English crown, visited the coast of Maine in the late 1490s.

Samuel de Champlain explored much of the Maine coast and present day Canada, in the service of the French government, in 1604.

the year 1000. John Cabot, an Italian explorer in the service of England, probably reached Maine in 1498. Then came the explorers sent by the French—Giovanni da Verrazano (1524); Pierre du Gua, Sieur de Monts (1604); and Samuel de Champlain (1604).

In 1605 George Weymouth, an Englishman, was sent to Maine to explore the coast. His reports were so favorable that his sponsors, Sir Ferdinando Gorges and Sir John Popham, established Popham Plantation near the mouth of the Kennebec River in 1607. The settlers built a ship, the *Virginia*, which was the first ship built by English colonists in the New World. But the cold weather forced them to return to England in 1608. Perhaps the first permanent settlement established in Maine by the English was near Saco, in 1623.

In 1622, the English crown gave Gorges and another Englishman, John Mason, a large piece of land in present-day Maine and New Hampshire, with Gorges being given the part that is now Maine. He established a government in 1636 and created the town of Georgeana (now York, the first chartered English town in what is now the United States) in 1641.

Gorges died in 1647, and the residents of Kittery, Wells, and York formed a new government. These people, plus the people of Casco Bay, Kennebunk, Saco, and Scarborough, voted to make Maine a part of the Massachusetts Bay Colony. In 1660 Gorges's heirs claimed that Maine still belonged to them, and in 1664, England ordered Maine to be returned. Massachusetts regained title to Maine in 1667—buying the territory for about $6,000. Between 1689 to 1763 many land skirmishes, including those of the French and

Indian Wars, were fought in Maine. When the French and Indian Wars ended, the French had given up their claims to most of North America, and Maine was English again.

Before the American Revolution, Maine men had their own "tea party," burning a supply of British tea at York in 1774. Hundreds of Maine men joined the Revolution to fight for freedom from English rule. A British blockade of Maine caused a shortage of food and other goods, and in 1775 the British burned Falmouth (now Portland). The first naval battle of the Revolution occurred off Machias in June 1775, when a group of Maine men captured the British ship *Margaretta*. Benedict Arnold and his colonial troops left Augusta to try to capture Quebec from the British, but they failed.

After the Revolutionary War, Maine's timber industry expanded, as did its shipping industry. The people voted for separation from Massachusetts, and Maine entered the Union as the 23rd state on March 15, 1820.

Maine was strongly against slavery before the Civil War. During the hostilities, about 72,000 Maine men fought on the Union side. After the war, the textile and leather industries of the state grew at a rapid rate. Toward the end of the 19th century, hydroelectric power came into use along the swift-running rivers of Maine.

The state suffered during the Great Depression of the 1930s, but conditions improved toward the end of that decade. About 95,000 Maine men and women served in the armed forces in World War II, and industries in the state made shoes and uniforms for the troops. Warships were built in Bath and South Portland. Since then, industry has continued to grow.

Windjammers, which were important as lumbering ships earlier this century, now often take passengers for cruises of Maine's coastal waters.

Sports

Maine's woods, lakes, and rivers have made the state a popular place for hunting and fishing. Downhill and cross-country skiing are popular in the winter. In the summer, many people enjoy cruising the state's extensive coastline in sail or motor boats.

Major Cities

Augusta (population 21,819). Settled in 1628, Augusta is the capital of Maine and is located at the head of navigation on the Kennebec River. It began as a trading post, established by men from the Plymouth Colony on the site of Cushnoc, an Indian village.

In 1754, Fort Western was built to protect the settlers from Indian raids. Today, some of the leading industries in the city are textiles, clothing, steel, and food processing. Things to see in Augusta include the statehouse (1829-32), the State Museum, and Blaine House.

White water rafting on Maine's inland rivers attracts many sports enthusiasts to the state.

The old port section of Portland, an area also known as the Old Port Exchange.

Lewiston (population 40,481). Settled in 1770, Lewiston is Maine's second largest city. Located 30 miles up the Androscoggin River from the sea, it is directly across the river from Auburn. A manufacturing town specializing in shoes, textiles, electronics, computers, and metal fabrication, Lewiston is the site of Bates College—New England's first coeducational institution of higher learning. Things to see in Lewiston include Mount David and the Treat Art Gallery.

Portland (population 61,572). Portland, which was settled in 1631, is Maine's largest city and is located on beautiful Casco Bay. It is a city with regal elm trees, stately houses, and historic churches. Before the Revolution, Portland was raided by the Indians several times, and during the war, in 1775, the British bombarded it, later burning it down. A fire wiped out large sections of the city in 1866, and poet Henry Wadsworth Longfellow said that the ruined town reminded him of Pompeii (an ancient city in southern Italy that was destroyed by a volcanic eruption).

Things to see in Portland include the Wadsworth-Longfellow House (1785), the Maine Historical Society, the Tate House (1755), Victoria Mansion (1858), the Portland Museum of Art, the Old Port Exchange, Portland Head Light (1791), and the Parson Smith House (1764).

The Portland Head Light is Maine's oldest lighthouse, built in 1791.

Places To Visit

The National Park Service maintains three areas in the state of Maine: Acadia National Park, part of White Mountain National Forest, and Saint Croix Island International Historic Site. In addition, there are 23 state recreation areas.

Auburn: Norlands Living History Center. This center is a village that shows farm life as it was lived a century ago.

Bailey Island: Bailey Island Bridge. This structure is built of uncemented granite rocks that let the tides flow between them.

Bath: Fort Popham Memorial. Here are the remains of an unfinished fort with its gun emplacements. Bath Maritime Museum. The history of Maine's ship building industry and commerce is exhibited in several buildings including a working shipwright's shed.

Bethel: Dr. Moses Mason House. Built in 1813, this house was the home of a congressman who served in the Jackson administration.

Blue Hill: Parson Fisher House. Designed and built in 1814 by the town's first minister, the Parson Fisher House contains his memorabilia.

Boothbay Harbor: Boothbay Railway Village. This village contains two restored railroad stations and an old-fashioned general store.

Brunswick: First Parish Church. This 1846 church contains the family pew of Harriet Beecher Stowe and the pulpit from which Henry Wadsworth Longfellow once spoke. Bowdoin College Museum of Art. The collection includes paintings by Winslow Homer and Andrew Wyeth.

Bucksport: Jed Prouty Tavern. Built in 1792 as a stagecoach stop, the tavern, which is still in operation, played host to Presidents Martin Van Buren, Andrew Jackson, William Henry Harrison, and John Tyler.

Camden: Old Conway House Complex. Here is a restored 18th-century farmstead, complete with farm implements and a blacksmith shop.

Damariscotta: Saint Patrick's Church. Built in 1808, this

The old mill in Brunswick is a reminder of the early nineteenth century, when waterpower made New England the manufacturing center of the United States.

The house in Brunswick where Harriet Beecher Stowe lived with her family while her husband was on the faculty at Bowdoin College.

Montpelier, the reconstructed home of General Henry Knox, in Thomaston.

brick church is the oldest Roman Catholic church in New England.

Farmington: Nordica Homestead. The birthplace of Lillian Nordica, the famous Wagnerian soprano, built in 1840, displays many of her costumes and other memorabilia.

Houlton: Market Square Historic District. The district is made up of a group of buildings dating from the 1860s.

Kennebunk: Taylor-Barry House. Built in 1803, the Taylor-Barry House was the home of a sea captain.

Kennebunkport: Seashore Trolley Museum. The museum contains some 150 antique streetcars from the United States and abroad.

Kittery: Sarah Orne Jewett House. Built in 1774, this house was the home of the author of *The Country of the Pointed Firs.*

Lubec: Roosevelt Campobello International Park. Jointly owned by the United States and Canada, this island park was once the summer home of President Franklin D. Roosevelt.

Machias: Ruggles House. This house, built in 1820 features delicately carved woodwork and an unusual "flying" staircase.

Ogunquit: Marginal Way. Marginal Way is a walk along the cliffs overlooking the ocean with tidepools at the water's edge.

Old Town: Old Town Canoe Company. This company is the only remaining production company in the United States making canoes.

Poland Spring: Shaker Museum. This museum consists of six buildings, one of them dating back to 1794, that contain furniture and other artifacts created by the Shakers, a 19th century religious sect.

Rockland: Owls Head Transportation Museum. The museum features working displays of antique cars, airplanes, and a huge steam engine.

Saco: Maine Aquarium. The aquarium contains more than 150 species of marine life, including seals, penguins, eels, sharks, and tropical fish.

Thomaston: Montpelier. Today's Montpelier is a reproduction of the house built by General Henry Knox, the Revolutionary War hero, in 1795.

Wiscasset: Nickels-Sortwell House. Built in 1807 for a sea captain, this house was later used as a hotel from 1820 to 1900. Musical Wonder House-Music Museum. A collection of music boxes and player pianos is displayed in a house built in 1852.

York: York Village. This section of York contains the Old Gaol (1720), the Emerson–Wilcox House (1742), Jefferd's Tavern (1759), The Old School House (1755), the Elizabeth Perkins House (1730), and the John Hancock Warehouse.

A pier in Wiscasset harbor leads to a float that rises and falls with the extreme tides of coastal Maine.

Events

There are many events and organizations that schedule activities of various kinds in the state of Maine. Here are some of them:

Sports: Fishing Tournament (Bailey Island), Kenduskeag Stream Canoe Race (Bangor), harness racing at Bass Park (Bangor), Great Adventures (Bingham), Tuna Tournament (Boothbay Harbor), 'Roostook River Raft Race (Caribou), Winter Sports Events (Fort Kent), Friendship Sloop Races (Friendship), Meduxnekeeg River Canoe Race (Houlton),

In Old Orchard Beach, where an annual art festival is held, the pier and lively boardwalk contribute to the pleasure of vacationers.

Spudland Open Golf Tournament (Presque Isle), Sled Dog Race (Rangeley), Maine Snow-Pro (Scarborough).

Arts and Crafts: Art Exhibit (Bar Harbor), Antique Show (Boothbay Harbor), Quilt Show (Bridgton), Garden Club Open House Day (Camden), Annual Art Festival (Old Orchard Beach), Sidewalk Art Show (Portland), Art Show (York), Antique Show (York), Craft Fair (York).

Music: Band concerts (Bangor), Bangor Symphony (Bangor), Bluegrass Festival (Brunswick), Brunswick Music Theater (Brunswick), Bowdoin Summer Music Festival (Brunswick), New England Music Camp (Waterville), Portland Symphony (Portland), Kotzschmar Memorial Organ Concerts (Portland).

Entertainment: Norlands Special Events (Auburn), Whatever Week (Augusta),

Bangor Fair (Bangor), Belfast Bay Festival (Belfast), Blue Hill Fair (Blue Hill), Fisherman's Festival (Boothbay Harbor), Windjammer Days (Boothbay Harbor), Obsolete Auto Show (Boothbay Harbor), Fall Foliage Festival (Boothbay Harbor), Winter Carnival (Bridgton), Winter Carnival (Caribou), Homecoming Week (Eastport), Franklin County Fair (Farmington), Chester Greenwood Day Celebration

(Farmington), Houlton Potato Feast (Houlton), Franco-American Festival (Lewiston), Indian Pageant (Old Town), Old Port Festival (Portland), Deering Oaks Family Festival (Portland), Northern Maine Fair (Presque Isle), Maine Lobster Festival (Rockland), Transportation Rally (Rockland), Skowhegan State Fair (Skowhegan), Skowhegan Log Day (Skowhegan), Clam Festival (Yarmouth).

Theater: Camden Amphitheatre (Camden), Ogunquit Playhouse (Ogunquit).

Famous People

Many famous people were born in the state of Maine. Here are a few:

Writers

Walter Van Tilburg Clark 1909-71, East Orland. Novelist: *The Ox-Bow Incident*

Tristram Coffin 1892-1955, Brunswick. Pulitzer Prize-winning poet: *Strange Holiness*

Sarah Orne Jewett 1849-1909, South Berwick. Novelist: *The Country of the Pointed Firs*

Stephen King b.1947, Portland. Novelist: *The Shining*

Henry Wadsworth Longfellow 1807-82, Portland. Poet: "Paul Revere's Ride"

Edna St. Vincent Millay 1892-1950, Rockland. Pulitzer Prize-winning poet: *The Harp Weaver and Other Poems*

The poet Henry Wadsworth Longfellow was the first American to be honored in the Poet's Corner of Westminster Abbey.

Walter Van Tilburg Clark, the author of The Ox-Bow Incident.

Kenneth Roberts 1885-1957, Kennebunk. Pulitzer Prize-winning novelist: *Northwest Passage*

Edward Arlington Robinson 1869-1935, Head Tide. Three-time Pulitzer Prize-winning poet: *Tristram*

Stephen King, a writer of best-selling horror novels.

Publishers and Journalists
Cyrus Curtis 1850-1933, Portland. Founder of Curtis Publishing Company
George Palmer Putnam 1814-72, Brunswick. Founder of G. P. Putnam & Sons publishing house

Inventors
Francis Stanley 1849-1918, Kingfield. Co-inventor of the Stanley Steamer automobile

Freelan Stanley 1849-1940, Kingfield. Co-inventor of the Stanley Steamer automobile

Religious Leader
Ellen Gould White 1827-1915, Gorham. Leader of the Seventh-Day Adventists

Government Officials
William Cohen b.1940, Bangor. United States senator
Hannibal Hamlin 1809-91, Paris Hill. Vice-president under Lincoln
Rufus King 1755-1857, Scarborough, Mass. (Now in Maine). United

Nelson Rockefeller, long-time governor of New York State, served as vice-president under Gerald Ford.

Margaret Chase Smith was the first woman to be elected to the U.S. Senate.

States senator and ambassador to Great Britain

Edmund Muskie b.1914, Rumford. Governor, United States senator, Secretary of State

Nelson Rockefeller 1908-79, Bar Harbor. Governor of New York and vice-president under Gerald Ford

Margaret Chase Smith b.1897, Skowhegan. United States senator

Military Figures

Oliver Otis Howard 1830-1909, Leeds. Civil War general and founder of Howard University

William Whipple 1730-85, Kittery. Revolutionary War leader and signer of the Declaration of Independence

Social Reformer

Dorothea Dix 1802-87, Hampden. Pioneer in specialized treatment of the mentally ill

Business Leaders

Charles A. Coffin 1844-1926, Somerset County. Founder of General Electric

William D. Washburn 1831-1912, Livermore. Founded Pillsbury Mills

Entertainer

Linda Lavin b.1937, Portland. Television actress: *Alice*

Director

John Ford 1895-1973, Cape Elizabeth. Five-time Academy Award-winning director: *The Quiet Man*

Colleges and Universities

There are many colleges and universities in Maine. Here are the most

Linda Lavin starred in the television series Alice.

prominent, with their locations, dates of founding, and enrollments.

Bates College, Lewiston, 1855, 1,516

Bowdoin College, Brunswick, 1794, 1,360

Colby College, Waterville, 1813, 1,746

Saint Joseph's College, Windham, 1915, 624

University of Maine, Orono, 1865, 11,145; *at Augusta*, 1965, 3,525; *at Farmington*, 1864, 2,358; *at Fort Kent*, 1878, 689; *at Machias*, 1909, 886; *at Presque Isle*, 1903, 1,428.

Where To Get More Information

Chamber of Commerce and Industry
126 Sewall Street
Augusta, ME 04330

New Hampshire

The first seal of New Hampshire was adopted in 1784, and was modified in 1931. The seal is circular, on a blue background. In the center is a reproduction of the Revolutionary War frigate *Raleigh*, surrounded by laurel to symbolize victory. Around the center is printed "Seal of the State of New Hampshire" with the date "1776," the year the state's first constitution was adopted. The outside ring of the seal contains nine laurel leaves alternating with stars.

New Hampshire also has a state emblem, adopted in 1945 and amended in 1957. The emblem is oval and contains a drawing of the Old Man of the Mountain (a rock formation in Franconia Notch State Park). Surrounding the drawing is the state motto at the bottom and the words *New Hampshire* at the top.

State Flag

The state flag, adopted in 1909 and modified in 1931, shows the state seal on a blue background.

State Motto

Live Free or Die

Adopted by the state legislature in 1945, these words were spoken by General John Stark as a toast at a veterans' reunion on July 31, 1809.

Scenic Newfound Lake in Bristol, New Hampshire.

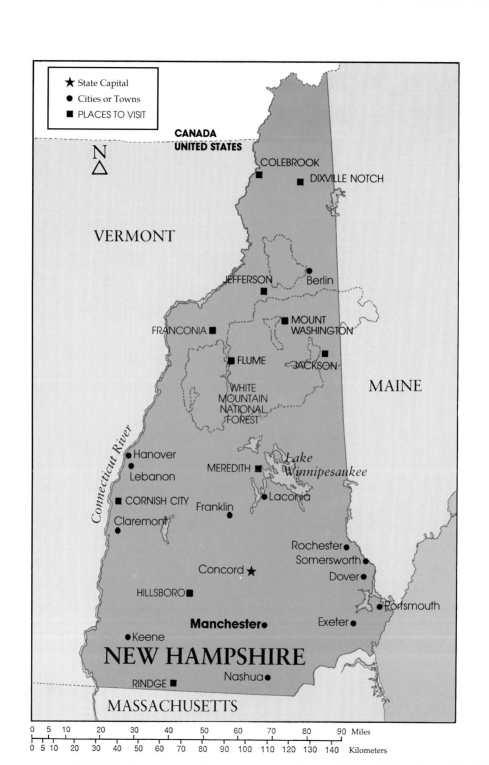

State Capital
Cities or Towns
PLACES TO VISIT

N

CANADA
UNITED STATES

COLEBROOK
DIXVILLE NOTCH

VERMONT

JEFFERSON
Berlin

FRANCONIA
MOUNT
WASHINGTON

FLUME
JACKSON

MAINE

WHITE
MOUNTAIN
NATIONAL
FOREST

Connecticut River

Hanover
MEREDITH
Lake
Winnipesaukee

Lebanon

CORNISH CITY
Franklin
Laconia

Claremont

Rochester
Somersworth
Dover

Concord ★

HILLSBORO
Portsmouth

Manchester
Exeter

Keene

NEW HAMPSHIRE

Nashua

RINDGE

MASSACHUSETTS

0   5 10   20   30   40   50   60   70   80   90 Miles
0 5 10 20   30   40   50   60   70   80   90 100 110 120 130 140 Kilometers

State Capital

Before New Hampshire became a state, the capital was first Portsmouth (1679-1774), then Exeter (1775-81), and finally Concord (1782-84). For the next several years the capital was in dispute, but Concord was finally selected as the permanent capital in 1808. The New Hampshire statehouse in Concord is the oldest state capitol in the United States in which the legislature uses its original chambers. Completed in 1819 at a cost of $82,000, the building is made of granite. Beginning in 1864 it was enlarged, and a new dome was added. It was enlarged again in 1909.

The statehouse in Concord is among the oldest in the United States.

State Name and Nicknames

England gave a grant to Captain John Mason of the Royal Navy in 1629, entitling him to a part of the New World that included what was to become the state of New Hampshire. Mason named the area for the British county of Hampshire, where he lived for much of his youth.

New Hampshire was nicknamed the *Granite State* because of the huge number of granite formations and quarries. It is also called the *White Mountain State* for the beautiful mountain range in the northern part of the state. The mountains also gave it another name, the *Switzerland of America*. The many rivers flowing from these mountains gave it yet another name, *The Mother of Rivers*.

State Flower

The purple lilac, *Syringa vulgaris*, was adopted by the legislature in 1919 after a

The purple lilac is the state flower.

long argument—the Senate wanting the purple aster and the House wanting the apple blossom. Finally, the purple lilac became the compromise choice.

State Tree

In 1947 the white birch, *Betula papyrifera*, was named the state tree at the urging of the New Hampshire Federation of Garden Clubs. This is the tree whose bark was used by the Indians to make their canoes, and it is found in huge numbers all over the state.

State Bird

Even though there were those who preferred the New Hampshire hen, the purple finch, *Carpodacus purpureus*, was named the state bird by the legislature in 1957.

The white birch is the state tree.

State Animal

Common to New Hampshire, the white-tailed deer, *Odocoileus virginianus*, was named the state animal in 1983.

New Hampshire

State Insect

The lady bug, *Adalia bipunctata,* was adopted as the state insect in 1977.

State Song

New Hampshire has two state songs. "Old New Hampshire," with words by Dr. John F. Holmes and music by Maurice Hoffman, was adopted by the state legislature in 1949. In 1963 "New Hampshire, My New Hampshire" was added. This song has music by Walter P. Smith and words by Julius Richelson.

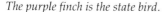
The purple finch is the state bird.

Squam Lake, one of the largest lakes in New Hampshire, is a popular vacation spot for fishermen.

Population

The population of New Hampshire in 1987 was 1,057,000, which makes it the 40th most populous state. There are 113.9 persons per square mile—52.2 percent of them in towns and cities. Almost all of the people of New Hampshire were born in the United States.

Geography and Climate

Bounded on the east by Maine and the Atlantic Ocean, on the south by Massachusetts, on the west by Vermont and the Canadian province of Quebec, and on the north by Quebec, New Hampshire has an area of 9,279 square miles, making it the 44th largest state. The climate is varied because of its high mountains and its nearness to the ocean.

New Hampshire has a short (18-mile) coastline, but most of the state consists of a central plateau with hills and mountains. The highest point in the state is on Mount Washington, at 6,288 feet above sea level, and the lowest point is at sea level, along the Atlantic Ocean. The major waterways in New Hampshire are the Connecticut, the Merrimack, the Androscoggin, the Saco, and the Piscataqua rivers. Lake Winnipesaukee is the largest lake in the state.

Industries

The principal industries of the state of New Hampshire are manufacturing, agriculture, and mining. The chief products are machinery, electrical and electronic products, plastics, fabricated metal products, and leather goods.

Agriculture

The chief crops of the state are dairy products, eggs, nursery and greenhouse products, hay, vegetables, fruit, maple syrup, and maple sugar products. New Hampshire is also a livestock state, and there are estimated to be some 55,000 cattle; 9,000 hogs and pigs; 12,000 sheep; and 365,000 chickens, geese, and turkeys

Sugar maples are tapped for syrup in the early spring.

on its farms. Sand, gravel, and stone are important mineral products. Commercial fishing brings in some $6.2 million each year.

Government

The governor is elected for a two-year term. There is no lieutenant governor. The state legislature, called the General Court, which meets every other year, has a senate of 24 members and a house of representatives of no less than 375 and no more than 400 members. These legislators are elected from the state's towns and wards (divisions of cities), which send from one to six legislators to the capital, depending on their populations. The state constitution was adopted in 1784. In addition to its two U.S. senators, New Hampshire has two representatives in the U.S. House of Representatives. The state has four votes in the electoral college.

Concord in 1852, at a time when New Hampshire was in the midst of an industrial boom.

History

Before the Europeans arrived in what was to become New Hampshire, there were about 5,000 Indians living in the area. Most of them were Abenaki Indians of the Algonkian Indian family. The Abenaki group included the Winnipesaukee, Pigwacket, and Pennacook bands. They all built their wigwams of bark and hides, and were hunters, fishermen, and farmers. Although they were peaceful Indians, they were attacked sometimes by the warlike Iroquois.

In the 1600s many explorers roamed the region, beginning in 1603, when the English explorer Martin Pring sailed his ship up the Piscataqua River from what is now Portsmouth. In 1605 Samuel de Champlain, the French explorer, landed on the coast. Then in 1614 English Captain John Smith

discovered the Isles of Shoals, naming them Smith's Islands.

King James I of England formed the Council for New England in 1620, which encouraged the settlement of the New World. In 1623, David Thompson was given land in present-day New Hampshire, and he and his followers settled at Odiorne's Point, which is now a part of Rye. Edward Hilton settled Hilton's Point, which is now Dover, in the 1620s. Strawbery Banke (now Portsmouth) was founded in 1630, and Exeter and Hampton in 1638.

In 1622, the British granted land in present-day New Hampshire and Maine to John Mason and Ferdinando Gorges. In 1629 the two men divided the territory, with Mason getting the part

Captain John Smith, the English explorer, landed on the Isles of Shoals in New Hampshire in 1614, during his exploration of the New England coast.

between the Merrimack and Piscataqua rivers, which he named New Hampshire, after his native English county—Hampshire. In 1641 New Hampshire was declared to be a part of Massachusetts, but in 1680 King Charles II of England made it a separate colony again.

From 1754 to 1761, the French and Indian Wars were fought in New England, with several battles taking place in New Hampshire. Two New Hampshire men, Robert Rogers (leader of Rogers' Rangers) and John Stark, were military leaders in these wars, which ended with the French giving up most of their holdings in the New World.

During the Revolutionary War, one of the first armed reactions by the colonists against British rule occurred when several New Hampshire men seized military supplies from the British fort at New Castle.

When the war broke out in Massachusetts in 1775, hundreds of New Hampshirites rushed to Boston to fight the British. But New Hampshire was the only colony in which no fighting took place *during the war*. On June 21, 1778, New Hampshire ratified the United States Constitution and became the ninth state to enter the Union.

Early in the 19th century New Hampshire began to manufacture textiles, and Portsmouth became a leading port for merchant ships. The first railroad was opened in 1838, and in 1846 Manchester became the state's first incorporated city. At midcentury New Hampshire was producing hosiery, woolen cloth, boots, shoes, machine tools, and wood products.

About 34,000 New Hampshire men served with the Union armed forces during the Civil War, and the Portsmouth Naval Shipyard built many blockade vessels for the Union Navy. After the war, industrial growth was spectacular. During World War I about 20,000 New Hampshire men were in the armed forces, and Portsmouth was again building naval ships.

New Hampshire's economic growth was slowed by the Great Depression of the 1930s, but then came World War II. Some 60,000 men and women from the state were in the armed forces during that war; the textile mills of the state were making uniforms; and Portsmouth was building submarines and warships.

Since then the state has become more urban and industrialized. And with the opening of many new highways and ski resorts, tourism has become an important activity. New Hampshire was also the first state to adopt a legal lottery, with the proceeds going to public education.

Camping attracts many visitors to New Hampshire's numerous state parks.

Sports

Like the other New England states, New Hampshire is known for its ski areas, especially those in the White Mountains. There is sailing on the coast and inland lakes. Fishing and hunting are also popular.

Major Cities

Concord (population 30,400). Settled in 1727, Concord became the state capital in 1808. It is the financial and political center of the state and also has much diversified industry. The legislature of New Hampshire is the largest in the United States. The state house contains portraits of famous people from New Hampshire. Visitors can also tour the New Hampshire Historical Society, the League of New Hampshire Craftsmen, the Pierce Manse and the Shaker Village in nearby Canterbury.

Manchester (population 90,936). Settled in 1722, Manchester was an industrial center in New Hampshire early on. But when its cotton textile industry failed in 1935, several New Hampshire citizens bought the plants, and this revived the town. Today the city has some 200 industries. Places to visit in Manchester include the Currier Gallery of Art, the Manchester Historic Association, and the McIntyre Ski Area.

Nashua (population 67,865). Settled in 1656, Nashua began as a fur-trading post. Early in the 19th century, the development of Merrimack River waterpower enabled Nashua to become an industrial center. Today this second largest city in the state has more than 100 industries ranging from computers and tools to beer. Travelers can visit Silver Lake State Park and the Nashua Center for the Arts and can tour the Anheuser-Busch Brewery, with its Clydesdale Hamlet in nearby Merrimack.

Places To Visit

The National Park Service maintains two areas in the state of New Hampshire: Saint-Gaudens National Historic Site and White

Mountain National Forest. In addition, there are 31 state recreation areas.

Claremont: Fort at N. 4. The Fort at N. 4. is a reconstruction of a fort used by colonists for defense in the French and Indian Wars.

Colebrook: Shrine of Our Lady of Grace. This 25-acre tract contains more than 50 Carrara marble and granite devotional monuments.

Cornish: Saint-Gaudens National Historic Site. Aspet was the home of the sculptor Augustus Saint-Gaudens and displays some of his work.

Dixville Notch: Table Rock. From this rock can be seen parts of New Hampshire, Maine, Vermont, and the Canadian province of Quebec.

Dover: Woodman Institute. This collection of museums includes the Dame Garrison House (1675) and the Woodman House (1818), now a natural history museum.

Exeter: Gillman Garrison House. This house is a renovated garrison (fortified against attack) house of log construction dating from 1690, with an 18th century wing.

Skiing has been a popular winter sport in New Hampshire since 1882, when the first U.S. ski club was founded in Berlin.

The Currier Gallery of Art in Manchester has one of the state's finest art collections.

Franconia: Frost Place. Visitors can see two furnished rooms in the house of the poet Robert Frost.

Franconia Notch State Park: Old Man of the Mountain. This natural formation in the White Mountains is a craggy granite likeness of a man's face, made famous in Nathaniel Hawthorne's short story "The Great Stone Face."

Franklin: Daniel Webster Birthplace. In this frame house, now restored, the statesman Daniel Webster was born in 1782.

Hanover: Dartmouth College. The Dartmouth campus has many fine white brick buildings, some of which date from 1784, also the Baker Memorial Library and the Hopkins Center for the Arts.

Hillsboro: Franklin Pierce Homestead. Built in 1804, this house is the restored childhood home of our 14th President.

Jackson: Heritage-New Hampshire. Thirty theatrical sets, with animation, sounds, and smells, illustrate 300 years of New Hampshire history.

Jefferson: Six Gun City. This is a Western frontier village with rides, a fort, an Indian village, and many other structures.

Keene: Wyman Tavern. Refurnished in 1820s style, the tavern was built in 1762.

Meredith: Winnipesaukee Railroad. The visitor can take scenic train rides in old railroad coaches along the shore of Lake Winnipesaukee.

Mount Washington: Cog railway. Visitors can ride up the west slope of the highest peak in the state.

Peterborough: Peterborough Toy Museum. This fine collection displays many types of antique toys.

Portsmouth: Strawbery Banke. This collection of 37 historic structures displays the history of Portsmouth from 1695 to 1945.

Rindge: Cathedral of the Pines. The Altar of the Nation in this international nondenominational shrine has been recognized by Congress as a memorial to all American war dead.

Events

There are many events and organizations that schedule activities of various kinds in the state of New Hampshire. Here are some of them.

Sports: Winter Carnival (Franklin), Yankee International Racing Federation of America, Inc. Regatta (Littleton), Winterfest (North Conway), Mountainfest (North Conway), Mount Washington Valley Equine Classic (North Conway), Mud Bowl (North Conway), Winter Carnival (Wolfeboro).

Arts and Crafts: Lakes Region Fine Arts and Crafts Festival (Meredith), Craftsmen's Fair (Sunapee).

Music: Band concerts (Hampton Beach), New Hampshire Music Festival (Laconia), New Hampshire Music Festival (Plymouth), Jazz Festival (Portsmouth), Prescott Park Arts Festival (Portsmouth), Festival of the Arts (Waterville Valley).

Entertainment: Lancaster Fair (Jefferson), Cheshire Fair (Kenne), SummerStreet (Littleton), Peterborough Festival Days (Peterborough), Plymouth State Fair (Plymouth), Rochester Fair (Rochester).

Tours: Tours of Dartmouth College (Hanover), InSight Tours (Portsmouth).

Theater: Hampton Playhouse (Hampton Beach), The Old Homestead (Keene), American Stage Festival (Nashua), Barn Playhouse (New London), Eastern Slope Playhouse (North Conway), Weathervane Theatre (Whitefield).

Mount Washington in New Hampshire is the highest peak in the northeastern United States.

Famous People

Many famous people were born in the state of New Hampshire. Here are a few:

Writers

Thomas Bailey Aldrich 1836-1907, Portsmouth. Editor and writer: *The Story of a Bad Boy*

John Irving b.1942, Exeter. Novelist: *The World According to Garp*

Newspaper publisher Horace Greeley was a noted abolitionist and popularizer of the slogan "Go west, young man."

John Irving is the best-selling author of The World According to Garp.

Grace Metalious 1924-64, Manchester. Novelist: *Peyton Place*

Architect

Ralph Adams Cram 1863-1942, Hampton Falls. Architect and medieval revivalist.

Artist

Daniel Chester French 1850-1931, Exeter. Sculptor

Publishers and Journalists

Harry Chandler 1864-1944, Landaff. *Los Angeles Times* publisher

Horace Greeley 1811-72, Amherst. Abolitionist editor of the New York *Tribune*

Philosopher and Religious Leader

Mary Baker Eddy 1821-1910, Bow. Founder of Christian Science

Explorer

Alan Shepard b.1923, East Derry. First U.S.

Mary Baker Eddy founded the First Church of Christ Scientist.

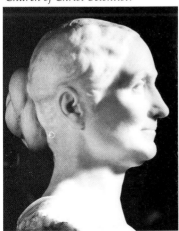

Daniel Webster, a senator known for his oratory, was a native of New Hampshire and a graduate of Dartmouth College.

astronaut to travel in space

Government Officials
Salmon P. Chase 1808-73, Cornish. Secretary of the Treasury under Lincoln
William Pitt Fessenden 1806-69, Boscawen. One of the founders of the Republican party
Franklin Pierce 1804-69, Hillsboro. Fourteenth President of the United States
Harlan Fiske Stone 1872-1946, Chesterfield. Chief Justice of the United States
Daniel Webster 1782-1852, Salisbury. United States senator and famed orator
Levi Woodbury 1789-1851, Francestown. United States senator and Supreme Court Justice

Military Figures
Benjamin Franklin Butler 1818-93, Deerfield. Union Army general
Fitz-John Porter 1822-1901, Portsmouth. Union Army general
Robert Rogers 1727-95, Dunbarton. Colonial officer in the French and Indian Wars
John Stark 1728-1822, Londonderry. Revolutionary War general
Leonard Wood 1860-1927, Winchester. U.S. Army general and governor-general of the Philippines

Social Reformer
Elizabeth Gurley Flynn 1890-1964, Concord. U.S. Communist leader

Business Leaders
George H. Bissell 1821-84, Hanover. Organizer of the first oil company, The Pennsylvania Rock Oil Co.

Salmon P. Chase, who served as Secretary of the Treasury, appears on the $10,000 bill.

William P. Cheney 1815-95, Hillsboro. Founder of the American Express Company

Ralph S. Damon 1897-1956, Franklin. President of TWA (Transworld Airlines)

John G. Shedd 1850-1926, Alstead. President of Marshall Field & Company

Sports Personality
Jane Blalock b.1945, Portsmouth. Championship golfer

Colleges and Universities
There are several colleges and universities in New Hampshire. Here are the most prominent, with their locations, dates of founding, and enrollment.

Dartmouth College, Hanover, 1769, 4,785

Keene State College, Keene, 1909, 3,205

New England College, Henniker, 1946, 1,062

Plymouth State College of the University System of New Hampshire, Plymouth, 1871, 3,999

Rivier College, Nashua, 1933, 1,584

Saint Anselm College, Manchester, 1889, 1,897

University of New Hampshire, Durham, 1866, 10,879

Where To Get More Information
New Hampshire Vacation Center
105 Loudon Road
P.O. Box 856
Concord, NH 03301
        or
Department of Resources and Economic Development
Office of Vacation Travel
P.O. Box 856
Concord, NH 03301

Dartmouth College, a member of the Ivy League, was founded in 1769.

Vermont

The original state seal was designed in 1779, but fell into disuse. Several other seals were used until 1937, when a modification of the original was adopted. Vermont's state seal is circular and is gold in color. In the center top is a pine tree with 14 branches, representing the original 13 states and Vermont. There are wavy lines at the top representing the sky and wavy lines at the bottom that stand for the sea. On the right of the tree is a cow representing dairying, and at the top of the tree, to the left and right, are sheaves of wheat, representing farming. Slightly below the center of the seal is the word *Vermont* and below that is the state motto: *"Freedom and Unity."*

Historic Groton, Vermont, lies in the foothills of the Green Mountians.

State Flag

The state flag, adopted in 1923, replaced previous state flags of 1803 and 1837. The coat of arms is centered on a blue background.

State Motto

Freedom and Unity

The motto first appeared on the state seal and indicated that the state should be free but united with the other members of the Union.

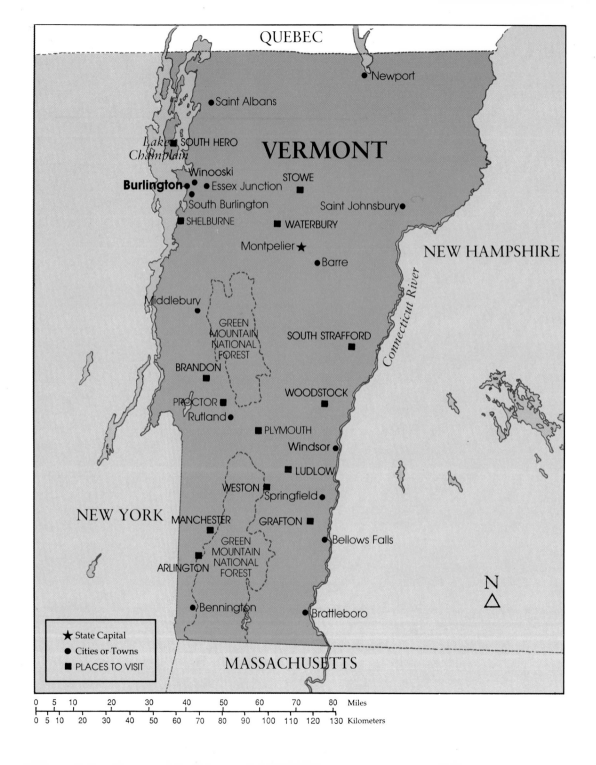